ABC of Behavioural Method

D1380142

The PACTS series: *Parent, Adolescent and Child Training Skills*

ABC of Behavioural Methods

by
Martin Herbert

BPS BOOKS THE BRITISH PSYCHOLOGICAL SOCIETY

First published in 1996 by BPS Books (The British Psychological Society), St Andrews House, 48 Princess Road East, Leicester LE1 7DR, UK.

A catalogue record for this book is available from the British Library.

ISBN 1 85433 195 7

Typeset by Ralph Footring, Derby.

Reprinted 1999

Contents

ABC of behavioural methods

Introduction

The *ABC of behaviour* is an acronym for some of the key elements in the analysis of children's behaviour – elements to do with the antecedents and consequences of behaviour, as well as other principles drawn from psychological learning theory. It also represents the notion of a problem-solving method for harassed parents beset with a child's difficult behaviour: a relatively simple way of thinking about child management which practitioners can impart to caregivers. I must stress that it is crucial for professionals who are novices in the use of behavioural methods to arrange supervision from an experienced behaviour therapist.

Aims

The aims of this guide are to provide practitioners with:

1. an introduction to the use of behavioural methods in order to alleviate childhood behaviour problems;
2. photocopiable material to give to parents as handouts, to be used as preliminaries to planning a programme for the child's behaviour problem(s);
3. a proforma for recording behaviour baselines and change;
4. a reading list on behavioural methods.

Objectives

When you have read this guide you should be familiar with:

1. the behavioural strategy of carrying out a so-called functional (ABC) analysis;
2. some of the behavioural tactics (methods) for changing behaviour;
3. the types of recording forms used in practice when monitoring behaviour change;
4. some of the key literature on the subject of behavioural work.

Part I: Learning to behave

The vast majority of a child's behaviours are learned and this includes the problematic ones that adults find so reprehensible or worrying. Children have to be taught how to behave 'normally'; that is, in a socially appropriate manner. To do anything well demands good training and involves two people: a learner and a teacher.

Parents, as teachers, are faced with a learner, their child, who has to learn all about social life and begins pretty well from scratch. Generally speaking, parents do not have the benefit of a formal training in parenthood, although they may have the enormous advantage of having had an informal induction by watching and helping their own parents.

Fortunately, we are not wholly dependent upon what we are taught; being human, we have a tremendous capacity to use our intuition and commonsense and work things out for ourselves. Without training in child-rearing, most parents do succeed in bringing up their offspring to be law-abiding, social adults.

Robust and adaptable as children are, it is not necessary for them to discover their way around their world entirely by trial and error. We can save them a lot of time, and circumvent some distressing mistakes, if parents prove to be wise guides and mentors. It must be emphasized that the ABC of learning theory only tells parents how to think about their own, and their child's behaviour; it shows them *how* to teach, not *what* to teach! Deciding what is desirable for youngsters is a question of individual parent values.

The nature of learning

When experience leads to a relatively permanent modification of behaviour, attitude or knowledge, we say that learning has occurred. Memorizing a formula, recognizing a face, reading music and being scared of maths or going to parties, are all examples of learning. We have to distinguish between *learning* an action or behaviour and actually *performing* it. Basically, in relation to the child, there are three preliminary questions to be answered.

1.   Does s/he know *what* to do?
2.   Does s/he know *how* to do it?
3.   Does s/he know *when* to do it?

Now, the child may know the appropriate behaviour or skill and when to produce it, but still may not perform it. So there are four more questions to be considered.

4.   How can I get him/her to do what I want him/her to do?
5.   Now that s/he does it, how can I encourage him/her to continue doing it?
6.   How can I get him/her to stop doing what I don't want him/her to do?
7.   Now that s/he has stopped doing it, how can I encourage him/her to desist from doing it?

The reason why we look at the Antecedents (see following) of a behaviour, that is, its cues or triggers, is that they are very important. If you think about, and watch, the settings of a child's behaviour, it may be that s/he behaves in a non-compliant way, or has a tantrum on some occasions but not others; that is, some situations seem to act as cues (antecedents) to them to behave in a particular way. People tend to tailor their behaviour to the particular places in which, and the different persons with whom, they find themselves, and in the case of children, this chameleon capacity often leads to misunderstandings between home and school with each blaming the other, when (more often than not) the child is difficult in one setting but not the other. A child tends to look around, consider the rules, the firmness of the adult, how other children behave, what is expected of him/her, and then decide how to behave.

The ABC of behaviour

This is where the ABC of behaviour will prove useful.

A   stands for *Antecedents* or what led up to the
B   which stands for *Behaviour* or what the child actually does, while
C   refers to the *Consequences* or what occurred immediately after the behaviour.

Meaningful stimuli (the antecedents) are vital because they direct our behaviour. Or to put this another way, it is crucial for the individual's survival that s/he *learns* to respond appropriately to stimuli. For instance, we can rely on most car drivers to respond to the stimulus of a red traffic light by stopping. If we could not, chaos would ensue. We can also depend on the vast majority of parents to respond to the stimulus of a crying child by caring for her/his needs, otherwise children would not survive.

Psychological laws often take the form of statements about the relationship between events. These are called stimulus–response (S–R) laws: 'Given stimulus Y, one would expect response Z'. Or more economically, 'If Y, then Z'. We can make use of these laws to make reasonable predictions about adult and child behaviour in given situations and conditions, thus putting us in a position to suggest ways of changing behaviour that has gone wrong. Many of the connections or associations between stimuli and responses are learned on the basis of imitation (modelling) or conditioning processes.

Modelling (imitation)

Experiments and observations have convincingly illustrated how children imitate, not only desirable behaviour, but also inappropriate behaviour. In one study, those nursery children who had observed aggressive models displayed a great number of precisely imitated aggressive responses, which rarely occurred in the other (control) group which had observed non-aggressive models. In addition, the results indicated that models observed on film were as effective as real-life models in transmitting hostile patterns of behaviour.

The example just given is a very simple one, but even such apparently simple patterns of learning are difficult to analyse. Psychologists are not certain why some models have an almost irresistible influence over children while others are ignored. Deficiencies in imitation may be due to inadequate attention to the modelled activities (one thinks here of the hyperactive child); inadequate retention of the stimuli ('I keep forgetting, Dad'); motor inadequacies ('I'm all fingers and thumbs with the sewing needle, Mum'); or lack of motivation ('I don't see why I should!'). With this type of learning (and with classical conditioning, which we will come to later) we are less concerned with the *consequences* of behaviour, than with the *antecedents* of behaviour; that is what goes before, or leads up to, the particular action. For example, a child might learn vicariously to fear a teacher because s/he has seen them treating another child harshly.

All of this is not to deny the importance of the **C** term (consequences) in observational learning. A child's actual performance of various socially-approved behaviours is given even greater impetus by praise and encouragement; in other words, they are reinforced by social (or symbolic) rewards. S/he will also be more likely to imitate if s/he sees that the model's actions have rewarding or prestigious consequences. Think of the many television characters, watched avidly by children, who achieve outcomes favourable to themselves by violent means!

These symbolic rewards regulate behaviour. The child is likely to be willing to obey distasteful rules because s/he wishes to have his/her parents' approval or avoid their disapproval. Their words of praise increase his/her self-esteem, and, in this way, s/he develops patterns of behaviour which conform to the social norm. Not all human behaviours require external reinforcements; children often learn to solve problems simply for the pleasure of solving them.

Applications

Modelling has been used successfully in treatment as we shall see in Part II. For example, masculine behaviours were taught to a boy who was being jeered at for his gender identity confusion – an effeminate style of walking, gesturing, sitting and so on. His misery evaporated as he acquired, by observational learning, more acceptably boyish mannerisms. Preschoolers have overcome their fear of dogs by watching another child pet, feed and play with a dog. Similar methods have helped children to master their terror of the dentist. Parents often model calm behaviour in the surgery for the benefit of their offspring, even sitting in the dentist's chair to indicate its safety.

Classical (respondent) conditioning

This is another form of learning which occurs on the '**A**' side of the ABC equation. Let us take a simple example. It would not be surprising if a dog responded to a slight pinprick to his leg by lifting and thus withdrawing his leg from the pinprick. The withdrawal of the leg is called a *respondent* and it is an example of an innate and involuntary behaviour (the withdrawal) elicited by a specific stimulus (the pinprick). It would be surprising if he responded in the same way to the sound of a bell. However, if an experimenter arranges that a dog regularly hears a bell, just prior to receiving a pinprick to his leg, the animal will, after several pairings of bell and pinprick, lift his leg to the bell alone! This is an example of classical conditioning. The conditioned response is formed when a stimulus (the bell), originally neutral with respect to a particular (and natural) response (lifting the leg), is paired a number of times with the stimulus eliciting that response (pinprick), so that the previously neutral stimulus itself (the bell) comes to elicit the response.

Classical conditioning can be seen at work, to take one example, in the development of phobic anxiety. The child who is bullied in the playground eventually feels fearful and manifests the symptoms of an anxiety attack at the mere sight of the playground, even in the absence of the bully.

Learning is not simply something that happens to the individual, but something which s/he makes happen by the manner in which s/he handles incoming information and puts it to use. The main difference between this model of learning and the ones we looked at earlier is that those methods do not pay enough attention to the element that comes in between, namely the learner's own behaviour (**B**). This behaviour is not simply something brought forth by a stimulus and strengthened, or otherwise, by the nature of the reinforcement that follows. It is, in fact, a highly complex activity which involves three major processes:

1.   the acquisition of information;
2.   the thoughtful manipulation or transformation of this information into a form suitable for dealing with the task in hand; and
3.   the testing and checking of the adequacy of this transformation.

Self-talk

What people say to themselves influences their behaviour. Faulty thinking can bring about 'faulty' actions, and may be revealed in what children tell themselves (self-talk). So changing by discussion and debate their self-talk, and, hopefully, their cognitions, will benefit the way they act and feel.

Now we have a different **ABC**, where **B** stands for the person's *beliefs* (perceptions, attributions, and so on) about a situation in which s/he finds him/herself.

A   stands for *Antecedent* events
B   stands for *Beliefs* (the meaning of the situation for the person)
C   stands for *Consequences* that flow from the person's *beliefs* and as they affect his/her *behaviour.*

Self-talk is a major preoccupation of all of us when we are beset with trials and tribulations: 'I can't cope any more … I'm in a terrible mess … There's no hope … Oh, what am I to do?' It is often accompanied by symptoms such as listlessness, weepiness, sleeplessness and social withdrawal and fear. A feeling of control is of particular importance in coping with fear; children can be taught to make statements to themselves such as 'I feel brave'; 'I *can* do it!', which help them, in turn, to manage their feelings.

Operant (instrumental) conditioning

Operant (or *instrumental*) conditioning describes a situation in which a person's behaviour is strengthened (that is, made more likely to occur in similar circumstances), because it was followed by a favourable consequence, that is to say, 'positive reinforcement'. It may, of course, be weakened by a punishing consequence.

Positive reinforcement

When, as we saw earlier, the consequence (the **C** term) of a behaviour is rewarding to a child, that behaviour is likely to increase in strength, and may even become more frequent! Put another way, if Clive does something, and as a result of his action something pleasant happens to him, then he is more likely to do the same thing in similar circumstances in the future. When psychologists refer to this pleasant outcome as the *positive reinforcement* of behaviour, they have in mind several kinds of reinforcers:

➤ *tangible* rewards (such as sweets, treats, pocket money);
➤ *social* rewards (such as attention, a smile, a pat on the back, a word of encouragement); and
➤ *self-reinforcers* (such as the ones that come from within and which are non-tangible – self-praise, self-approval, a sense of pleasure).

For instance, if you say 'Clive, that was nice of you to let Sally have a turn on your bike, I am very pleased with you', Clive is more likely to lend his bicycle again. (Note: we are dealing in *probabilities*, not certainties.)

Here, then, is that form of learning – *instrumental* or *operant conditioning/learning* – in which the frequency of a behaviour which occurs quite spontaneously in the individual is increased by following its appearance with a reward; that is, by reinforcing it. If it does not occur spontaneously, you will have to *prompt* it, and then *reinforce* it. If the interval is too long, learning does not occur. It is of little use promising a young child a reward for some good deed which won't materialize for a week; it is not likely to have much incentive or teaching value. Long deferred punishments, likewise, are ineffectual. Of course, older children are better able to understand delayed incentives. Symbolic rewards such as stars, stickers, or happy faces on a chart (see *Appendix IV*), bridge the gap between action and a promised reward (say, a football match).

In day-to-day situations, it is only on the odd occasion that a parent says 'good boy' or smiles in approval when his/her child behaves appropriately or well. In fact, there is evidence that what is referred to as *intermittent reinforcement* (the occasional reward) is a more potent method for maintaining the frequency of desirable behaviour than reinforcement presented for every 'correct' response made. The manufacturers of 'one armed bandits' (fruit machines) have cleverly used this principle in the schedules of reinforcement programmed into the machines. You win just often enough to keep you at that machine.

We know that it can be helpful to look at difficult behaviour by analysing very precisely the behaviour itself, what led up to it and what happened immediately before *and* after.

The 'when–then' rule

The reward should *follow* the desired action, not precede it. This has been called Grandma's Rule: '*When* you've washed the dishes, *then* you can play outside'. Not the other way around.

What the clinicians are looking for in trying to understand why the child behaves in a certain way, is the relationship between the individual's own activity and the rewarding results it produces; those behaviours (in this case, attention-seeking disruptive behaviour) that lead to satisfying consequences tend to be repeated under similar circumstances.

I have often heard a mother say, as this one did, 'Carol must be allergic to me. The very moment she sees me she plays up, no matter how good she's been with other people before I appeared on the scene'. Technically speaking, the mother's presence represents what is called a *discriminative stimulus* for Carol's disruptive behaviour. A discriminative stimulus is a kind of marker; it signals to the child the availability of reinforcers – lots of lovely rewarding attention.

Negative reinforcement

Behaving in a manner that *avoids* an unpleasant outcome leads to the reinforcement of behaviour, thus making it more likely to recur in similar circumstances.

Positive and negative reinforcement techniques give parents and teachers four training methods: *reward training*; *privation training*; *escape training*; and *avoidance training*. These can be summarized as follows:

➤ *Reward training:* 'If you do the desirable thing, I will give you a reward.'

➤ *Privation training:* 'If you don't do the desirable thing, I will withdraw a reward.'

➤ *Escape training:* 'If you do the desirable thing, I will withdraw a penalty.'

➤ *Avoidance training:* 'If you don't do the desirable thing, I will give you a penalty.'

Part II: The assessment

Identification and specification of the problem

The preliminary information in an assessment of behaviour problems often comes from parents, and they tend to report their children's problems in terms of rather vague and global labels such as 'tantrums', 'disobedience', 'rebelliousness', or 'aggressiveness'. The parent is encouraged to give descriptive examples of the problem, in other words, to define what s/he means in specific and observable terms when s/he uses a particular label. The clinician's brief will be (*inter alia*) to pinpoint problematic behaviours, attitudes, beliefs and interactions in terms of examples of what people **do** and **say**; to examine contingencies (the ABC of behaviour/beliefs); to put these into a *developmental* framework which takes account of *family dynamics;* to teach parents/child to observe (and possibly record) interactions; and then to discuss the data/information fully with them – that is, to arrive at a shared clinical formulation.

Steps towards identifying and specifying the problem

Following is a verbatim account of several examples of problem behaviour, providing not only a specified, measurable definition of what the problem is but also giving the context of antecedent and consequent events which will be useful during the next phase of the assessment.

Step 1. Identify and pinpoint the problems

Practitioner: Would you like to tell me in your own words what is worrying you – the concerns you would like us to help you with? Don't feel you have to hurry; take your time. (Pause at suitable intervals to summarize what the client has said.) I would like to pause for a moment to see whether I've understood properly the points you have made.

Practitioner (later): Are there any other matters you'd like to go into? Thank you for that helpful account. I can see that you are worried. I would like to clarify some of the points you have made by asking you for some other examples of your child's behaviour.

Step 2. Identify the child's assets

Practitioner: You have pointed out some of your problems with your child. If we look at this form you will see that it has a Credit and Debit column. I've listed on the debit side all of her/his behaviours that you find unacceptable; now let us list the good points on the credit side. (LATER) …

I want you to take this form home and look out for pleasant, helpful and other positive things that your child does, and note them down. I will also ask you to observe her/his negative behaviours on another form so that we can study them together and work out a plan of action.

Step 3: Identify desired outcomes (broad goals)

Practitioner: If I had a magic wand and could wave it and give you three wishes so that your child's behaviour was different, what would you wish to change? **OR**

If you were to wake up one morning to find that your child had changed for the better, how would you know? What would be different about his/her behaviour or attitude?

Step 4: Specify the target behaviours

Practitioner: The behaviours you wish to change are sometimes called 'target behaviours'. This is for the ABC of behaviour which we will discuss. The B term stands for **behaviour** (your child's temper tantrums in this instance), and it also stands for **beliefs** (your feelings and attitudes about what is happening in this instance). Let us be clear about what you are going to observe at home and elsewhere. So what is it that s/he **does** and **says** that makes you call her/his actions and words a 'temper tantrum'?

Step 5: Observe how frequently s/he loses her/his temper

Practitioner: I want you to count the number of tantrums, defined by those actions you described, that your child has each day; that is, the number of episodes. You could also time how long each episode lasts. Do this over three or four days.

Step 6: Look at the ABC of Behaviour *(see record form in Appendix III)*

Practitioner: I want you to keep a brief diary record of each episode, with particular emphasis on the ABC sequence:

A   What led up to the
B   TANTRUM? and
C   What happened immediately afterwards?

Step 7: Analyse your information, beginning with the antecedents

Practitioner: When you look at your diary after a few days, and at your tally of tantrums, are they part of a more general pattern? Are the As, the antecedents, rather similar?

Parent: Yes, they seem to form a pattern of defiance. They follow two lines; either my child tells me to do something, and if I don't she insists and eventually has a tantrum. Or I ask her to do something, she ignores me, or says 'I won't!', and if I insist she has a tantrum.

Step 8: Find out how specific the tantrums are

Practitioner: When you look at your tally, do the tantrums seem more frequent:

1.   at certain times?
2.   in certain places?
3.   with certain people?
4.   in particular situations?

Parent: The answer in this case is yes to all those questions. They are most frequent in the morning and at night; in the bedroom, at the dinner table; with me; when I try to dress her; get her to eat up her meal; or put away her toys.

Step 9: Formulation: analysing the antecedents and consequences

Practitioner: Do you think you may have slipped into the habit of simply repeating your commands like a broken record over and over again, without really expecting any results? Do you always give way, perhaps because it's the easiest thing to do? Looking at your diary again, can you see any kind of pattern in the Cs (the consequences or outcomes), to these trying confrontations?

Parent: Yes. Jane usually gets her own way ... not always but nearly always. She also gets me going. I sometimes end up in tears. She always gets me into an argument and I have to devote a lot of time to the dispute.

Practitioner: Who were you really observing? The answer inevitably will be not only your child. You are observing, as part of your analysis of As and Cs, your child in relation to yourself *and* others. It is not possible to understand a child's behaviour without looking at the influence of other people on her, and her influence on them.

Practitioner: In this instance, you (and others) have unwittingly reinforced (strengthened) the very behaviours (tantrums) that you wished to reduce in frequency. For example, one reinforcer is that she gets her own way; the second is that she riles you and enjoys winding you up; the third reinforcer is that she monopolizes your attention; even if it is scolding, it is rewarding. You know that it is rewarding and not punishing because the behaviour is as persistent as ever.

Step 10: Identify precise intervention (programme) goals

Practitioner: Be quite clear in your mind how Jane might change in order for the situation to improve. Also be specific. For example, 'I expect her to obey me when I make a reasonable request or command, so that if (say) I ask her to put her toys away, she does so without endless arguments or fits of temper'.

Part III: Behavioural methods

This guide is not only about changing the undesirable behaviour of 'problem children' but also about altering the behaviour of the people – parents, teachers and others – who form a significant part of the child's social world. Help is directed to the modification of that environment, rather than withdrawing the child from it. The parents become the real agents of change, thus contributing to the problem of extending positive changes over time. At the back of this book (*Hints for Parents*, p. 29) there is some guidance in a form that can be given to parents, preferably as a basis for discussion with the practitioner, as a preliminary to some planned change-strategies.

There are two important themes underlying the approach recommended in the guide.

1. The therapeutic *process* is one based on partnership, the 'collaborative' model of working. It is designed to empower parents and engender a mood of optimism where previously there was 'learned helplessness' (see Webster-Stratton and Herbert, 1994).
2. The therapeutic *content* of the approach, which allows for such optimism and a genuine therapeutic partnership, is based on social learning theory (see Herbert, 1993).

The collaborative model

The collaborative approach includes the following processes.

➤ *Negotiation.* The key question is, 'How are we *together* going to address the problems? It means engaging the person(s) in planning shared work toward treatment goals.

➤ *Education.* This involves the clarification of ideas about the disorder, its characteristics and treatment. It means providing explanations, empowering parents by giving reasons, sharing information and increasing knowledge. It is helpful to mention examples of other people's success, despite the difficulties, engendering a mood of optimism.

➤ *Observation.* Clients are encouraged and helped to observe their own (and their child's) reaction to the methods used, and shown how to record them during treatment.

➤ *Behaviour rehearsal.* Clients are given the opportunity to practise, in an atmosphere where they feel comfortable and unthreatened, coping skills (for example, relaxation skills, self-talk and anger/impulse control), child management skills (such as giving instructions, being consistent), and social skills.

➤ *Self-talk rehearsal.* Clients are encouraged to rehearse positive 'coping' statements, for example, 'I can manage'; 'I can cope with this situation'; 'Stay calm, breathe slowly, quietly'.

➤ *Eliciting support.* If necessary, if possible, and if the client permits, other members of the family, or outside helpers are brought in as aides.

➤ *Demythologizing.* It is often necessary to counter the myths and attributions that get in the way of therapeutic change. Parents' perceptions of their offspring, and their ideologies and attributions with regard to child rearing, make for an important area of assessment and discussion.

Some myths and unhelpful attributions

Here are some typical examples of myths and unhelpful attributions.

Sole ownership
➤ It's my child's problem; s/he's the one who has to change.
➤ It's me who's to blame.

If it doesn't hurt, it doesn't work
➤ A good belting is all s/he needs.
➤ Kindness doesn't work with him/her! All s/he understands is a good hiding.

Narrow limit-setting
➤ Give her/him an inch and s/he takes a mile.

Broad limits
➤ S/he won't love me if I insist.
➤ I feel so guilty if I say no.

Gender issues
➤ Only fathers can set firm limits.
➤ It's a mother's job, the discipline side of things.

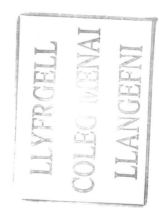

Scapegoating
➢   It's his/her father's bad blood coming out in her/him.

Attributions
➢   There's a demon in her/him.
➢   I don't trust him; he has his father in him.

Catastrophizing
➢   I'm a complete failure as a parent.
➢   I can't forgive myself for the mistakes I've made.

Intergenerational ideas
➢   The hidings I had from my father did me no harm, so they won't do her/him any harm.

The application of a collaborative programme depends, for its effectiveness, on a clear explanation of *what* is involved, and *why* the methods are likely to work (that is, their rationale). Ideas about problem-solving, resolving 'unfinished emotional business', facing change, and resisting it, are discussed. The following are some of those issues.

Your child is trying to solve a life problem

Practitioner: Rather than thinking of your child as *having* a problem or *being* a problem, it may help to think of her/him as trying to solve a problem. That behaviour you don't like may be her/his way of trying to deal not very successfully (for after all s/he's a learner) with one of life's difficulties. Let us try to see what s/he is trying to achieve. What are the developmental tasks s/he has to solve at this stage of life?

Laying ghosts to rest (reframing)

Practitioner: You may be finding it difficult to put all your thought and energy into the present difficulty. Perhaps there are some 'ghosts' from the past (things you blame yourself for needlessly in your child-rearing) that still haunt you. Let us try to put them to rest by talking about them, as then you may feel more confident about facing the future.

Putting on a new set of 'goggles'

Practitioner: We all find it difficult to change; indeed, it can be painful. We get used to the figurative 'goggles' or 'glasses' through which we look at the world in general, and our child in particular. To have to put on a different set of goggles can be quite confusing at first. We feel comfortable with what's familiar, so a new perspective is strange and rather scary. But that feeling soon wears off.

Change is not without cost

Practitioner: You find it difficult to give up the anger and resentment you feel all the time for your youngster's past misdemeanours. Let's try to see why it is so hard. We'll make two columns with the headings 'Advantages' and 'Disadvantages' of letting go of the anger.

Parent:	Advantages	Disadvantages
	I'd feel better.	It would look as if his/her behaviour was unimportant to me.
	I'd feel less tense.	I'd lose my self-respect.
	Be more rational.	People may think I don't care in my rearing of my children.

Practitioner: You can see that there are some good reasons, to your mind, in **NOT** giving up your anger. So change is costly. What you need to think through are the relative costs of changing, as opposed to not changing.

The treatment agenda is not only about 'correctives' to antisocial behaviour. Parents need principles and practical techniques for encouraging and maintaining not only compliant, but also other prosocial behaviours. In relation to this point it is important to advocate on behalf of the children and check on what is being asked of them, and on what has, or has not, been taught them. Children can hardly be blamed for not doing what they don't know, are not capable of, or see to be deviant. The seven questions listed on p. 3 are pertinent here.

The *Hints for Parents* at the end of this guide describe briefly some of the main methods to deal with these issues, couched in a form that can be presented collaboratively to parents; in other words, they can think about them for themselves in relation to their children. These methods represent a *tactical* approach to behaviour management. Also important are the more broadly based *strategic* methods which I will describe next.

Teaching parents to teach their children to problem solve

How do young children with conduct problems typically react to their problems? By crying, hitting, swearing, running away, refusing to do as they are told, or tattling to their parents. These responses do not usually lead to solutions; in fact, they create new problems. Of course, all children will exhibit these responses to conflict, but research has indicated that when presented with interpersonal problem situations, conduct-problem and rejected children find it difficult to consider alternative courses of action. They search for fewer clues or facts and generate fewer appropriate solutions to conflict situations. They produce a higher percentage of aggressive and incompetent solutions than do co-operative children, and have a more difficult time anticipating the consequences of their solutions. They act aggressively and impulsively without stopping to think of non-aggressive solutions. On the other hand, there is evidence from research that young children who employ a wide range of alternative and competent strategies on problem-solving tasks tend to play more constructively, are better liked, and are less aggressive. Therefore the purpose of this component of the programme is for the therapist to teach parents how they can teach their children appropriate problem-solving skills.

Questions parents ask about problem solving

Shouldn't you tell children the correct solutions?

'I feel I need to tell my children how to solve the problem because they don't come up with the right answer on their own — in fact, some of their own solutions are really bad!'

Is there such a thing as too little guidance?

'Well, I just tell my children to work it out on their own. I think that's the only way children will learn to problem-solve. Don't you agree?'

Feelings don't have much to do with problem-solving, do they?

'I don't talk much about feelings with my children. What value is there in this?'

Many parents believe that telling their children how to solve a problem helps them learn to problem-solve. For example, two children may have trouble sharing a bicycle. The parent responds to the child who grabbed the bicycle from the child who refused to share the bike by saying, 'You should either play together or take turns. Grabbing is not nice. You can't go around grabbing things. Would you like that if s/he did it to you?' The problem with this approach is that the parents are telling the children what to do before they have found out what the children think the problem is. It is possible, after all, that the parent has misdiagnosed the problem. For example, in this case it was not entirely the fault of the child who grabbed the bicycle because the other child had used the bike for a long time and had refused to share it even when asked nicely. As the child continued to refuse to share, the other child resorted to grabbing. Moreover, the parents' approach in this example does not help the children to think about their problem and how to solve it. Rather than being encouraged to learn how to think, they are *told* what to think, and the solution is imposed upon them.

The opposite problem occurs when parents think they are helping their children resolve a conflict by telling them to work it out for themselves. This might work if the children already have good problem-solving skills; but for most young children this approach will not work. For example, if Max and Terry are fighting over a book, non-intervention will probably result in continued arguing and Terry, the more aggressive child, getting the book. Therefore, Terry is reinforced for his inappropriate behaviour because he got what he wanted, and Max is reinforced to giving in because the fighting ceased when he backed down.

Here are the main points we emphasize:

➤ Help children define the problem.
➤ Talk about feelings.
➤ Involve children in brainstorming possible solutions.
➤ Be positive and imaginative.
➤ Model creative solutions.
➤ Encourage children to think through the possible consequences of different solutions.
➤ Remember that it is the process of learning how to think about the conflict that is critical, rather than getting 'correct' answers.

You might suggest that the parents begin to teach their children these skills by role playing or acting them out with puppets or books. Recommend that these discussions occur at neutral times, not in the heat of battle. Once parents have taught children the steps and the language to talk about problems, they can then begin to help them learn how to use the skills in the midst of real conflict.

It is effective for parents to guide their children into thinking about what may have caused the problem in the first place, rather than telling them the solution. Parents can invite their children to come up with possible solutions; if parents want to help children develop a habit of solving their own problems, they need to be asked to think for themselves. Parents can encourage their children to talk aloud as they think and then can praise their ideas and attempts at solutions. In this way the parents are reinforcing the development of a style of thinking that will help their child deal with all kinds of problems throughout their lives. Parents need to encourage their children to first come up with many possible solutions and they can then help them to shift their focus to the possible consequences of each solution. The final step in problem-solving is to help children evaluate their possible solutions. For children aged three to nine years, the second step, generating solutions, is the key skill to learn. While older children are more easily involved in anticipating consequences and evaluating them, youngsters need to be helped to generate possible solutions and to understand that some solutions are better than others. They should be urged to express their feelings about the situation, talk about ideas for solving the problem, and talk about what might happen if they carried out various solutions. The only time parents need to offer solutions is if their children need a few ideas to get them started.

The therapist should emphasize the importance of parental modelling as a way to teach children problem-solving skills. It is a rich learning experience for children to watch parents discussing problems with other adults, negotiating and resolving conflict, and evaluating the outcomes of their actions. While parents may not want their children to observe all their discussions, many daily interactions provide good opportunities for children to learn. For instance, children learn much of their behaviour by observing how parents react to life's daily hassles. They learn from noticing how their parents say 'No' to a friend's request. They watch with interest how Dad receives Mum's suggestion to wear something different. Is Mum sarcastic, angry, or matter-of-fact in her request? Does Dad sulk, get angry, co-operate or ask for more information? Watching parents decide which TV film to watch on Saturday night can teach much about compromise and negotiation. Parents can help further by thinking out loud their positive problem-solving strategies. For example, a parent might say, 'How can I solve this? I need to stop and think first. What plan can I come up with to make this successful?'

Teaching parents to think strategically

We have looked at some of the basic methods based on the ABC approach. Here, briefly, are some further strategic methods for parents to think about for themselves in relation to their children.

Natural consequences

If parents ensure, within the limits of safety, that the child is allowed to experience the consequences of his/her own actions, this becomes an effective means of modifying behaviour. If a child is rough with a possession and, for example, it breaks, s/he is more likely to learn to be careful if s/he has to do without it. If parents always replace the toy, s/he is likely to continue to be destructive.

Unfortunately, from the point of view of the parents' 'self-interest', children are frequently not left to experience the consequences of their own misdeeds. Against their own, and the child's, best interests they intervene to 'protect' their offspring from reality. Potentially educative (though punishing) reality is replaced by a kind parent; the result, however, of this kindness is that the implications (outcomes) of the situation often do not become apparent to the child and they go on repeating the same misdeeds over and over again. A good deal of discussion and debate with parents, particularly over-protective ones, is required here. The issue is, to what extent, particularly with toddlers and teenagers, should parents intervene (interfere?) to protect the child from the inevitable risks of life? To what extent is the child allowed to learn from experience?

Self-management training

In order to engender or to strengthen self-control, techniques have been developed to help change the parent's or child's instructions to him/herself. Training involves raising the client's consciousness of the circumstances in which s/he gets angry; and then moves through a series of stages. First the therapist models the performance of a task, making appropriate and positive self-statements, for example, 'Think first, act afterwards'; 'It's not worth losing my temper'; 'I'll count to ten and stay calm'. The client then practises the same behaviour, gradually moving to whispered, and eventually to silent, self-instruction. Clients are encouraged to use self-statements so that they can observe, evaluate and reinforce appropriate overt behaviours in themselves.

A variation in modifying self-statements is the self-talk analysis and training applied to the individual beset with trials and tribulations – 'I can't cope any more ... I'm in a terrible mess ... There's no hope ... Oh, what am I to do?', or whose self-statements are exaggerated – 'No-one loves me ... there's no hope!', or illogical in the sense that they suggest a need to be all-competent, show no weaknesses, be acknowledged and loved *all* the time, to be forever right, or to be forever in the wrong.

The therapist attempts, in conversation with the client, to expose the faulty reasoning underlying the self-talk and to provide arguments and statements that counter and defuse the distressing situation.

Making use of contracts

It may sound distinctly odd, if not demeaning, to parents to consider negotiating a written agreement with a child or using business-style contracts to resolve family conflicts. Surely these are the domain of lawyers or salesmen and far too cold and commercial to apply to human relationships? But it is precisely because a contract *is* such a detached, objective way of dealing with emotional issues that sitting down as a family to draft an agreement can be effective. It is not only the content of the contract that is important; the *process* of arriving at the agreed terms can be therapeutic.

In coercive families, the cues or messages are frequently negative ones, the 'sound and fury' of criticism, nagging, crying, shouting and hitting out being the norm. Communication between members may be not so much aversive as impoverished or practically non-existent. Where family systems include behaviour control by the use of verbal and/or physical pain, they are likely to produce children who exhibit a high rate of aggressive actions. Coercive interactions, maintained by negative reinforcement, are most likely to operate in close social systems where the child must learn to cope with aversive stimuli such as incessant criticism.

This is where contracts come in. They can be used to 'open' closed systems. And certainly, one way of increasing positively reinforcing communications while reducing punitive interactions, is by sitting down to work out a contract with members of the family. The discussion, negotiation and compromise in such therapist-led situations introduces the family to an important means of resolving interpersonal conflicts and tensions and to enhanced communication, which they may have experienced only rarely.

The following guidelines might be followed in planning the contract.

➤ Keep the discussion positive. Recriminations are unavoidable, but the volume should be kept down and negative complaints turned into positive suggestions.

➤ Be very specific in spelling out desired actions.

➤ Pay attention to the details of privileges and conditions for both parties. They should (a) be important, and not trivial, and (b) make sense to the person involved.

➤ Encourage positive and specific actions if the parent wishes her/his child or partner to desist from certain activities.

➤ Choose changes the clients want to bring about that can easily be monitored. If one can't see whether an obligation has been met, one can't readily grant a privilege.

➤ Make clear to all concerned the penalties for breaking the contract.

➤ Keep a diary of progress. It is helpful, during the contract discussion period, if family members write down five specific things they'd like to see changed.

➤ The contract drawn up must embody the principles of mutual caring. If it doesn't, it is likely to fail.

References

Callias, M. (1994). Parent training. In M. Rutter, E. Taylor, and L. Hersov (Eds) *Child and Adolescent Psychiatry*. Oxford: Blackwell Scientific.

Ollendick, T.H. (1986). Behaviour therapy with children and adolescents. In: S.L. Garfield and A.E. Bergen (Eds) *Handbook of Psychotherapy and Behavior Change*, 3rd edn. New York: John Wiley.

Webster-Stratton, C. and Herbert, M. (1994). *Troubled Families – Problem Children: Working with Parents: a collaborative process*. Chichester: Wiley.

Further reading

Herbert, M. (1987). *Behavioural Treatment of Children with Problems: Practice Manual*, revised edn. London: Academic Press.

Herbert, M. (1993). *Working with Children and the Children Act: A practical guide for the helping professions*. Leicester: BPS Books (The British Psychological Society).

Herbert, M. (1987). *Living with Teenagers*. Oxford: Basil Blackwell.

Herbert, M. (1987). *Conduct Disorders of Childhood and Adolescence: A social learning perspective*, revised edn. Chichester: Wiley.

Herbert, M. (1988). *Discipline: A Positive Approach for Parents*. Oxford: Basil Blackwell.

Appendix I: An illustration of a functional (ABC) analysis

1. *Antecedent events*
   (possible precipitants)

   Carlton is asked to do something
   or to stop doing it.

2. *Behaviour*
   (a) Non-compliance. He takes no
   notice; if his mother insists, he
   resorts to verbal abuse.

   (b) Verbal abuse. He makes rude
   comments, criticizes, occasionally
   swears and shouts.

3. *Consequences*
   (possible reinforcers)
   (a) Mother shouts at him, scolds
   him or discusses at length with
   him what he has done.

   (b) She begs him.

   (c) Usually he gets his own way.

Specificity of Carlton's responses

Persons: He's rude and
             disobedient mainly with
             his mother; occasionally
             to his father; never with
             his grandmother.

Places: Anywhere (but notably
             when visiting, or at a
             supermarket).

Times: Meals in particular – at
             the beginning, usually, of
             the family meal.

Situations: Mainly when asked to do
             something or when
             challenged over being
             late for meals or for bad
             manners. Particularly
             when questioned about,
             or criticized for, not
             eating properly, getting
             up and leaving the table.

Appendix II: Frequency Chart

Child's name:
Date:
Week beginning:

Target behaviours: Symbol:
1. _____   _____
2. _____   _____
3. _____   _____

	Monday	Tuesday	Wednes-day	Thurs-day	Friday	Saturday	Sunday
6–8 a.m.							
8–10 a.m.							
10–12 a.m.							
12–2 p.m.							
2–4 p.m.							
4–6 p.m.							
6–8 p.m.							
8–10 p.m.							
10–12 p.m.							
12–2 a.m.							
2–4 a.m.							
4–6 a.m.							

Appendix III: Child's ABC Record Chart

Child's name:
Child's age:
Caregiver's name:
Date:

Behaviour being recorded:

Date and time	Antecedents: what happened beforehand?	Behaviour: what did your child do?	Consequences: what was the end result? (i) What did you do (e.g. ignore, argue, scold, smack, etc.)? (ii) How did s/he react?	Describe your feelings

Appendix IV: Sticker Chart

A sticker or happy face is applied for each task successfully achieved.

Name:

	Task			Week			Remarks
Monday							
Tuesday							
Wednesday							
Thursday							
Friday							
Saturday							
Sunday							

	Task			Week			Remarks
Monday							
Tuesday							
Wednesday							
Thursday							
Friday							
Saturday							
Sunday							

Hints for Parents

Learning to behave

The vast majority of a child's behaviours are learned and this includes the problematic ones that we adults find so reprehensible or worrying. Children have to be taught how to behave 'normally'; that is, in a socially appropriate manner. To do anything well demands good training and involves two people: a learner and a teacher.

We parents, as teachers, are faced with a learner, our child, who has to learn all about social life and who begins pretty well from scratch. Generally speaking, we do not have the benefit of a formal training in parenthood. Fortunately, we are not wholly dependent upon what we are taught; being human, we have a tremendous capacity to use our intuition and common sense and work things out for ourselves.

Robust and adaptable as children are, it is not necessary for them to discover their way around the world entirely by trial and error. We can save them a lot of time, and circumvent some distressing mistakes, if we as parents prove to be wise guides and mentors. Basically, in relation to your child, there are three preliminary questions to be answered:

1. Does s/he know *what* to do?
2. Does s/he know *how* to do it?
3. Does s/he know *when* to do it?

Now your child may know what the appropriate behaviour or skill is, and when to produce it, but still not perform it. So there are four more questions to consider:

4. How can I get him/her to do what I want him/her to do?
5. Now that s/he does it, how can I encourage him/her to continue doing it?
6. How can I get him/her to stop doing what I don't want him/her to do?
7. Now that s/he has stopped doing it, how can I encourage him/her to desist from doing it?

This is where the **ABC** of behaviour will prove useful.

A   stands for *Antecedents* or what led up to the
B   which stands for *Behaviour* (or what the child actually does), while
C   refers to the *Consequences* (or what occurred immediately after the behaviour).

Meaningful environmental 'signals' or stimuli (the **A** term) are vital because they direct our behaviour. Or to put this another way, it is crucial for our survival that we *learn* to respond appropriately to stimuli. For instance, most of us respond to the stimulus of a red traffic light by stopping. If we did not, chaos would ensue. Likewise, most parents will respond to the stimulus of a crying child by caring for her/his needs, otherwise children would not survive.

Positive reinforcement

If the consequence of a behaviour is rewarding (that is, favourable) to a child, that behaviour is likely to increase in strength, and may become more frequent! Put another way; if Clive does something, and as a result of his action something pleasant happens to him, then he is more likely to do the same thing in similar circumstances in the future. When psychologists refer to this pleasant outcome as the 'positive reinforcement' of behaviour, they have in mind several kinds of reinforcers: *tangible* rewards (for example, sweets, treats, pocket money); *social* rewards (for example, attention, a smile, a pat on the back, a word of encouragement); and *self-reinforcers* (that is, the ones that come from within and which are non-tangible – self-praise, self-approval, a sense of pleasure). For instance, if you say 'Clive, that was nice of you to let Sally have a turn on your bike, I am very pleased with you', Clive is more likely to lend his bicycle again. (Note: we are dealing in *probabilities* not certainties.) There is not much point in promising a young child a reward which they won't get for a week, as this is not likely to have much incentive or teaching value. Of course, older children are better able to understand delayed incentives. Symbolic rewards, such as stars or stickers on a chart, help to bridge the gap between action and a promised reward (say, a football match at the end of the week).

It can be helpful to look at difficult behaviour by analysing very *precisely* the behaviour itself, what led up to it and what happened immediately before *and* after.

The 'when–then' rule

The reward should *follow* the desired action, not precede it: '*When* you've washed the dishes, *then* you can play outside'. Not the other way around.

What clinicians are looking for in trying to understand why a child behaves in a certain way, is the relationship between the child's activity and the rewarding results it produces. Those behaviours, even attention-seeking disruptive behaviour, that led to satisfying consequences tended to be repeated under similar circumstances.

Are you making your child's behaviour worthwhile?

Some parents remember to reward (or in psychologist's jargon *reinforce*) desirable behaviour as in the following example.

Antecedents	Behaviour	Consequences
Patrice was asked to put away her toys.	She did so.	Her mum gave her a big hug and said thank you.

Patrice is likely to tidy up her toys when asked again. However, some parents persistently overlook or ignore their children's desirable actions, as in the following example.

Antecedents	Behaviour	Consequences
James asked his brother, Dennis, for a turn on his new bike.	Dennis got off and helped James on to the bike.	Nil! Mother made no comment. James rode off without a word of thanks.

It won't be surprising if Dennis doesn't share his things next time around.

Some parents unwittingly make undesirable behaviour worthwhile:

Antecedents	Behaviour	Consequences
David was told to leave the television off.	He kept putting it on.	It was eventually left on – to give people a bit of peace.
Aisha was having breakfast.	She kept getting down from her place.	Mum followed her round with a bowl of cereal, feeding her with a spoonful whenever she could.

In both of these instances, the child's unacceptable actions were rewarded by the child getting his/her own way. In other words, the child received positive reinforcement for behaving in an undesirable manner, which made it even more likely to occur again.

Some parents make undesirable behaviour unworthwhile:

Antecedents	**Behaviour**	**Consequences**
Johnnie wanted to go to the park; Dad said there wasn't time before tea.	Johnnie kicked and shouted, lay on the floor and screamed.	Dad ignored his tantrum; eventually Johnnie calmed down and began to play.

Negative reinforcement

Behaving in a manner that *avoids* an unpleasant outcome leads to the reinforcement of behaviour, thus making it more likely to recur in similar circumstances. If a child does something you do not like, such as losing his/her temper too easily, you may *increase* his/her ability to think first and hold his/her temper, by penalizing him/her consistently for failing to do so; in this way you are providing what is called 'negative reinforcement' for his/her efforts to 'keep his/her cool'. You may not have to apply the penalty if s/he believes your threat because of your record of keeping your word. For instance, if you say, 'Donna, if you do not think first, but lash out at your sister, I will not allow you to watch the television', then her resolve to think first and desist from hitting out will be strengthened.

Strengthening new behaviour patterns

Positive reinforcement

In order to improve or to increase your child's performance of certain actions, arrange matters so that an immediate reward follows the correct performance of the desired behaviour. You might indicate your intentions by saying, for example, '*When* you have put your toys away, *then* you can go out'. The 'when–then' formula reminds you that you only reward after the desired action is carried out. When the child has learned a behaviour it is no longer necessary to give rewards regularly. Remember that words of praise and encouragement at such a stage can be very reinforcing.

Developing new behaviour patterns

Encouragement

Secure your child's co-operation by guiding and helping him/her towards some desirable action or way of thought. Use a combination of suggestion, appreciation of his/her difficulties, praise for his/her efforts, and pleasure at his/her success.

In order to encourage your child to act in a way in which s/he has seldom or never before behaved, reward attempts at the correct action. You can take your child through mini-steps towards a goal by rewarding any action that comes close to the behaviour you want and continuing to reinforce the attempts at the behaviour you wish to elicit. No reinforcement is given to 'wrong' behaviours. Gradually make your standards (criteria) for your child's attempts more and more stringent until, in the end, s/he is only rewarded for the precise behaviour that is required.

Modelling

In order to teach your child a new pattern of behaviour, give him/her the opportunity to observe a person who is significant to him/her performing the desired behaviour. For example, if your child finds it hard to share, prompt one of their friends to demonstrate co-operative behaviour.

Skills training (for example, behaviour rehearsal)

Simulate real-life situations in which skills are to be developed. During rehearsal:

1. demonstrate the skill;
2. ask your child to practise the skill, using role play or providing a model if necessary;
3. provide feedback as to the accuracy/inaccuracy of his/her performance (if possible, video equipment is most useful here to evaluate the effectiveness of his/her own performance);
4. give homework assignments, for example, real-life planned practice of skills. Not only does behaviour rehearsal provide for acquiring new skills but it also allows their practice at a controlled pace and in a safe environment, and in this way minimizes distress.

Cueing

In order to train your child to act at a specific time, arrange for him/her to receive a cue for the correct performance just before the action is expected, rather than after s/he has performed incorrectly.

Discrimination

In order to teach your child to act in a particular manner under one set of circumstances but not another, train him/her to identify the cues that are different between the appropriate and inappropriate circumstances. Reward him/her only when his/her action is appropriate to the cue (for example, s/he is praised for crossing the pedestrian crossing when the signal is given).

Maintaining new behaviour (intermittent reinforcement)

In order to encourage your child to continue performing an established pattern of behaviour with few or no rewards, decrease the frequency with which the correct behaviour is rewarded, gradually and intermittently.

Stopping inappropriate behaviour (satiation)

To get your child to desist from acting in a particular way, allow (or make) him/her to continue performing the undesired act until s/he tires of it. Of course this will not be appropriate if the act is dangerous or seriously antisocial. If s/he tears up your curtains, give him/her bundles of newspapers to tear up until s/he is thoroughly bored with it. Psychologists have asked older children to 'practise' a tic energetically for five minutes several times a day. This makes a child more aware of his/her bad habit and helps him/her to inhibit it.

Reduction of the behaviour

To stop your child from acting in a particular way, arrange conditions so that s/he receives no rewards following the undesired acts. Ignore minor misdemeanours such as whining, pestering, tantrums. If a child grabs toys or other goodies from his/her small brother, try to ensure that grabbing has no rewarding outcome. Return the toy to its owner. (You could combine the training that grabbing is unproductive with the teaching of *sharing* to the younger child, and saying 'please'/waiting patiently to the older child. Encourage them to take turns.)

Withhold reinforcements such as approval, attention, and the like, which have previously and inappropriately followed inappropriate behaviour. **Remember**: your child may 'work hard' to regain the lost reinforcement and thus may get 'worse' before s/he gets 'better'. If the problem behaviour has been continuously reinforced in the past, then extinction should be relatively swift; after all, it is much easier for the child to recognize that s/he has lost reinforcers than it is for the child on intermittent reinforcement. In the latter case, extinction tends to be slow.

Planned ignoring

This is suitable for behaviours such as temper tantrums and whining and includes:

1. turning away or walking away from your child, as soon as the misbehaviour begins;
2. saying nothing and trying not to show any expression at all;
3. resisting getting into any debate, argument or discussion with your child while s/he is misbehaving.
4. if you think s/he deserves an explanation for whatever is upsetting him/her then say to him, 'When you have calmed down, we will talk about it'.

Time-out

This procedure is intended to reduce the frequency of an undesirable behaviour by ensuring that it is followed by a reduction in the opportunity to acquire reinforcement or rewards. In practice one can distinguish three forms of time-out:

1. **Activity time-out** where your child is simply barred from joining in an enjoyable activity, but still allowed to observe it – for example, having misbehaved s/he is made to sit out of a game.
2. **Room time-out** where s/he is removed from an enjoyable activity, not allowed to observe this, but not totally isolated, for example standing outside a classroom having misbehaved.
3. **Seclusion time-out** where s/he is socially isolated in a situation from which s/he cannot voluntarily escape.

Time-out sometimes leads to tantrums or rebellious behaviour such as crying, screaming, and physical assaults, particularly if the child has to be taken by force to a quiet room. With older, physically resistive children the method may simply not be feasible, so the procedure and its choice requires careful consideration.

When the behaviour to be eliminated is an extraordinarily compelling one that demands attention (reinforcement) from those present, or when time-out is difficult to administer because the child is strong and protesting, an equivalent of time-out may be instituted by removing the sources of reinforcement from him/her. So if you are a major source of reinforcement you could remove yourself, together with a magazine, to the bathroom, locking yourself in when your child's temper tantrums erupt and coming out only when all is quiet.

The child is warned in advance about those of his/her behaviours that are considered inappropriate and the consequences that will follow from them. Time-out may last from three to five minutes. In, practice, 'activity' or 'room' time-out should always be preferred before any form of 'seclusion' time-out.

A critical determinant of the effectiveness of time-out is the extent to which your child actually enjoys the situation from which s/he is removed. If that situation is positively frightening, anxiety-provoking or boring, it is possible that the time-out procedure might involve removing the child to a less aversive situation and thereby actually *increase* rather than decrease, the frequency of the inappropriate behaviour.

Overcorrection (restitutional overcorrection)

Requires your child to correct the consequences of his/her misbehaviour. Not only must s/he remedy the situation s/he has caused, but must also 'over-correct' it to an improved or better-than-normal state. In other words, you enforce the performance of a new behaviour in the situation where you want it to become routine.

Overcorrection (positive practice)

Get the child to practise positive behaviours which are physically incompatible with the inappropriate behaviour. For instance, a child who steals and breaks another youngster's penknife is required to save up enough money not only to replace the knife, but also to buy a small gift showing their regret. The child is praised once they have done so. A child who deliberately punctures another child's bicycle tyre not only has to repair the tyre but also must oil and polish the entire bicycle.

Positive reinforcement (promotion of alternative behaviour)

This involves positively reinforcing a particular type of behaviour which is inconsistent with, or which cannot be performed at the same time as, the undesired act. In other words, to stop a child from acting in a particular way, deliberately reinforce a competing action. For example, busying a child's hand with packing goods into shopping bags keeps them from putting unwanted items into the shopping trolley on the other side of the check-out counter.

Negative reinforcement

To stop your child from acting in a particular way, arrange for him/her to terminate a *mildly* unpleasant situation immediately by changing his/her behaviour in the desired direction. For example, every time they throw their toys in a dangerous manner the offending toys are locked away in a box for a week. S/he can avert this by heeding your warning. This penalty system is called *response cost* (see following).

Response cost, or fining

This procedure achieves a reduction in the frequency of an undesirable response by ensuring that its occurrence results in the removal of things which the youngster is known to value. In practice it usually involves removing rewards or incentives according to a predetermined 'tariff', or fines or sanctions, after the occurrence of an inappropriate behaviour. For example, Peter is always pulling items off the supermarket shelf when he goes shopping with his mum. Prior to entering the supermarket she explains to him that he is not to touch items on the shelves, and he is to hold on to the shopping trolley with one hand, and in the other hand, he can carry around a bar of chocolate. Every time he touches an item on the shelves the chocolate bar has a piece removed. (Note: it is necessary to get a child to repeat the instructions to check that they have understood them.)

At home, a jar of marbles (each one representing a unit of pocket money) can provide a visible reminder of the 'cost' of reprehensible behaviour. Add in some extra marbles so that your child can earn a bonus by desisting from (say) offensive remarks. It is important to be precise about what the penalty is for, namely that one marble is removed each time they are rude. No arbitrary changes in the penalty system should be introduced!

Conclusion

It is hoped that you will find some of these methods helpful. The trick is:

1. to stay calm;
2. to think before you act;
3. to work out what problem your child is trying to solve by being so 'problematic';
4. to use the appropriate management method.

As a backdrop to your disciplinary practices always remember:

1. to catch out your child in *good* behaviour, not only bad behaviour;
2. to praise and encourage whenever you can;
3. to try to provide your child with as much special (quality) time as you are able.